# A BEGINNER'S GUIDE TO DAILY GRATITUDE PRACTICE

# A BEGINNER'S GUIDE TO DAILY GRATITUDE PRACTICE

*Cultivating Joy and Abundance in Your Life*

JESS WILLIAMS

*Dedicated to all those who seek to transform their lives through the power of gratitude.*

# Contents

# Introduction

∞ ∞ ∞

Welcome to *"A Beginner's Guide to Daily Gratitude Practice: Cultivating Joy and Abundance in Your Life,"* where we will explore the transformative power of gratitude and how it can change your life. Have you ever felt like something is missing in your life, even though you have everything you need? Or perhaps you find yourself constantly focusing on the negatives, rather than the positives? If so, then you are not alone. In today's fast-paced and stressful world, it is easy to get caught up in the daily grind and forget to appreciate the blessings that surround us.

Gratitude is the practice of acknowledging and appreciating the good things in our lives. It is a simple yet powerful tool that can help us shift our mindset from scarcity to abundance, from fear to love, and from stress to peace. By cultivating a daily gratitude practice, we can transform our lives in profound ways and experience more joy, fulfillment, and inner peace.

In this short book, I will guide you through the process of starting and maintaining a daily gratitude practice. I will share with you the latest research on the science of gratitude and how it affects our brain and our overall well-being. You will learn how to use gratitude to attract more abundance and joy into your life, deepen your relationships, and even manifest your desires.

Through this book, I will provide you with simple yet effective techniques that you can incorporate into your daily routine to cultivate gratitude. You will learn how to start a gratitude journal, practice gratitude meditations, and use gratitude affirmations to shift your mindset and attract more positivity into your life.

I believe that gratitude is a transformative practice that can benefit everyone, regardless of their background or life circumstances. By cultivating a daily gratitude practice, we can transform our lives and experience more joy, abundance, and inner peace. I invite you to join me on this journey of gratitude, and to experience the many benefits that it can bring to your life.

# I

# Understanding the Power of Gratitude

∞ ∞ ∞

In this chapter, we will explore the science behind gratitude and how it affects our brain and overall well being. Gratitude has been shown to have numerous benefits, both physical and psychological. It can boost our immune system, improve our sleep, and reduce our stress levels. Moreover, gratitude can also increase our feelings of happiness, contentment, and overall life satisfaction.

Recent studies have shown that practicing gratitude can actually rewire our brains, changing the way we perceive the world and ourselves. Gratitude activates the release of dopamine and serotonin, the feel-good neurotransmitters in our brains, which help us feel happier, more content, and less anxious. Additionally, gratitude can increase our resilience to stress and help us cope better with life's challenges.

Together we will unveil the different ways gratitude can benefit our lives. We will also look at some inspiring stories of people who have transformed their lives through the practice of gratitude. These stories will illustrate how gratitude can help us overcome adversity, improve our relationships, and find meaning and purpose in our lives.

One example of how gratitude can transform our lives is the story of Tony Robbins. As a young man, Robbins struggled with depression and poverty. He was living in a small apartment and barely making ends meet. One day, he decided to shift his focus from what he lacked to what he had. He started a gratitude practice, where he would write down three things he was grateful for each day. Over time, this practice helped him change his mindset and attract more abundance and success into his life. Today, Robbins is a world-renowned motivational speaker and a multimillionaire.

Through stories like Tony's, we can see how the practice of gratitude can help us transform our lives and achieve our goals. By cultivating a daily gratitude practice, we can shift our mindset from scarcity to abundance, from fear to love, and from stress to peace. In the following chapters, we will explore how to start and maintain a daily gratitude practice and use gratitude to attract more abundance and joy into our lives.

Gratitude is a powerful emotion that has been scientifically proven to have many benefits for our brain and overall well-being. When we feel grateful, our brain releases neurotransmitters such as dopamine and serotonin, which are associated with feelings of pleasure, happiness, and well-being. This creates a positive feedback loop that reinforces our feelings of gratitude and happiness.

Studies have shown that people who practice gratitude regularly have better mental health, lower levels of stress and anxiety, and improved sleep quality. They are also more resilient to negative emotions, such as depression, anger, and frustration. By focusing on the positive aspects of their lives, grateful people are able to cultivate a more optimistic and positive outlook on life. You get what you give.

One of the ways gratitude affects our brain is by activating the prefrontal cortex, the part of the brain that is responsible for executive functions such as decision-making, problem-solving, and emotional regulation. This region of the brain is also involved in social cognition, which means that gratitude can help us improve our social interactions and relationships. Grateful people are more empathetic, compassionate, and forgiving, which makes them more likable and trustworthy.

Gratitude can also have a positive effect on our physical health. Studies have shown that people who practice gratitude have lower levels of inflammation, which is associated with a variety of chronic diseases, such as heart disease, diabetes, and cancer. Additionally, grateful people are more likely to engage in healthy behaviors, such as regular exercise and a balanced diet, which can further improve their physical health.

In summary, gratitude is a powerful emotion that can have many positive effects on our brain and overall well-being. By practicing gratitude regularly, we can improve our mental and physical health, enhance our social relationships, and cultivate a more positive and optimistic outlook on life.

Gratitude is a powerful practice that can benefit our lives in many different ways. In addition to the physical and mental health benefits, gratitude can also improve our relationships, increase our sense of purpose and meaning, and help us achieve our goals.

One of the ways gratitude can improve our relationships is by fostering feelings of empathy, compassion, and forgiveness. When we feel grateful for the people in our lives, we are more likely to treat them with kindness and respect. We are also more likely to forgive them when they make mistakes or hurt us. This can lead to stronger and more fulfilling relationships with our loved ones.

Gratitude can also increase our sense of purpose and meaning in life. When we focus on the positive aspects of our lives, we are more likely to see the bigger picture and appreciate the journey we are on. This can help us feel more fulfilled and satisfied with our lives, even in the face of adversity. This also sends more vibrations back to you on the same frequency. The universe wants to give you more things to feel grateful for!

Finally, gratitude can help us achieve our goals by keeping us motivated and focused on what we want to achieve. When we feel grateful for the progress we have made, we are more likely to continue working towards our goals. Gratitude can also help us attract more abundance and success into our lives, as we focus on the positive aspects of our lives and open ourselves up to new opportunities.

There are many inspiring stories of people who have transformed their lives through the practice of gratitude. For example, Oprah Winfrey has spoken about how gratitude has helped her overcome difficult times in her life and achieve her goals. In her book "The Wisdom of Sundays," she writes, "I know for sure that appreciating whatever shows up for you in life changes your personal vibration. You radiate and generate more goodness for yourself when you're aware of all you have and not focusing on your have- nots."

Another example is the story of Aisha Chaudhary, who was diagnosed with a rare genetic disorder at the age of 13. Despite her illness, Aisha remained grateful for the time she had with her family and the opportunities she had to make a difference in the world. She became an inspirational speaker and author, sharing her message of hope and gratitude with others.

These stories and many others demonstrate the power of gratitude to transform our lives, even in the face of adversity. By cultivating a daily gratitude practice, we can experience the many benefits of gratitude and live more fulfilling and satisfying lives.

# II

Starting Your Daily
Gratitude Practice

∞ ∞ ∞

We will now dive into a range of simple yet powerful techniques that you can use to cultivate gratitude on a daily basis. These techniques include gratitude journaling, gratitude meditations, and gratitude affirmations.

Gratitude journaling is a popular technique for cultivating gratitude. It involves taking a few minutes each day to write down a list of things that you are grateful for. This can be as simple as three things that happened during your day that you are grateful for, or as complex as a detailed reflection on a significant event or person in your life. The act of writing down your gratitude can help you focus your attention on the positive aspects of your life and develop a more positive mindset.

Gratitude meditations are another powerful technique for cultivating gratitude. These meditations can be as short as a few minutes or as long as you like. They involve focusing your attention on the present moment and expressing gratitude for the things that you have in your life. By cultivating a sense of gratitude and appreciation, you can reduce stress, anxiety, and depression, and improve your overall sense of well-being.

Gratitude affirmations are a simple yet effective technique for cultivating gratitude. Affirmations are positive statements that you repeat to yourself to help you cultivate a positive mindset. Gratitude affirmations can be as simple as "I am grateful for my health" or "I am grateful for my family and friends." By repeating these affirmations regularly, you can shift your focus from negative thoughts and feelings to positive ones.

*TIP: Leave yourself sticky notes with some of your favorite affirmations to get in the habit of repeating them.*

In addition to these techniques, this chapter will also provide guidance on creating a daily gratitude practice that works for you. We will explore different ways of incorporating gratitude into your daily routine, such as practicing gratitude in the morning, before bed, or throughout the day. We will also provide tips for staying motivated and making your gratitude practice a habit.

By the end of this chapter, you will have a solid understanding of how to start your daily gratitude practice and the many benefits that it can bring to your life. You will also have a range of practical techniques and strategies that you can use to cultivate gratitude on a daily basis, helping you to live a happier, more fulfilling life.

In Chapter 1, we explored the power of gratitude and how it can transform your life. Now, it's time to put that knowledge into action and start your daily gratitude practice.

### Why Start a Daily Gratitude Practice?

Before we dive into the techniques, let's take a moment to reflect on why starting a daily gratitude practice is so important. Research has shown that gratitude can have a range of benefits for our mental, emotional, and physical health. Here are just a few of the ways that gratitude can benefit your life:

1. Increased happiness: When we focus on the good things in our lives, we are more likely to feel happy and content.
2. Reduced stress: Gratitude can help reduce stress and anxiety, which can have a range of benefits for our overall health.
3. Improved relationships: Expressing gratitude to the people in our lives can help strengthen our relationships and foster feelings of love and connection.
4. Better sleep: Gratitude has been shown to improve sleep quality and reduce insomnia.
5. Increased resilience: Cultivating gratitude can help us bounce back from difficult situations and cope with stress more effectively.

Now that we know why gratitude is so important, let's explore some techniques for starting your daily gratitude practice.

**Technique 1:** *Gratitude Journaling*
Gratitude journaling is one of the most popular techniques for cultivating gratitude. It involves taking a few minutes each day to write down a list of things that you are grateful for. Here's how to get started:

1. Set aside a few minutes each day to journal. This could be in the morning, before bed, or at any other time that works for you.
2. To start, use the journaling sheets available to you in this book. Once you get comfortable with this method, get a dedicated journal or notebook that you enjoy writing in.
3. Write down three things that you are grateful for. These can be big or small, and can include anything from the people in your life to the simple pleasures of your day.

4. Take a moment to reflect on each item and why you are grateful for it.
5. Repeat this process every day.

Gratitude journaling is a simple yet powerful technique for shifting your focus to the positive aspects of your life.

**Technique 2:** *Gratitude Meditations*
Gratitude meditations are another powerful technique for cultivating gratitude. They involve focusing your attention on the present moment and expressing gratitude for the things that you have in your life. Here's how to get started:

1. Find a quiet place where you can meditate without distractions.
2. Sit comfortably with your eyes closed.
3. Take a few deep breaths and focus on your breath.
4. Begin to bring to mind the things that you are grateful for.
5. Visualize each thing and express gratitude for it in your mind.
6. Repeat this process for as long as you like.

Gratitude meditations can help reduce stress, anxiety, and depression, and improve your overall sense of well-being.

**Technique 3:** *Gratitude Affirmations*
Gratitude affirmations are a simple yet effective technique for cultivating gratitude. They involve repeating positive statements to yourself to help you cultivate a positive mindset. Here's how to get started:

1. Choose a few gratitude affirmations that resonate with you. Examples include "I am grateful for my health," "I am grateful for my family and friends," or "I am grateful for the abundance in my life."

2. Repeat these affirmations to yourself throughout the day, either silently or out loud.
3. Take a moment to reflect on each affirmation and feel the gratitude in your heart.

Gratitude affirmations can help shift your focus from negative thoughts and feelings to positive ones, helping you to feel happier and more motivated.

In conclusion, starting a daily gratitude practice is a simple yet powerful way to transform your life. By focusing on the positive aspects of your life and cultivating feelings of gratitude, you can improve your overall well- being, increase your resilience to stress and adversity, and enhance your relationships with others.

Remember, gratitude is a mindset that can be developed with practice. By incorporating gratitude journaling, gratitude meditations, and gratitude affirmations into your daily routine, you can begin to experience the many benefits of a regular gratitude practice.

In the next chapter, we will explore how to use gratitude to overcome challenges and achieve your goals. So, let's continue on this journey of transformation together.

# III

# Using Gratitude to Overcome Challenges and Achieve Your Goals

∞ ∞ ∞

Gratitude can help you overcome challenges and stay committed to your goals. We will discuss the role of gratitude in increasing your resilience and motivation, and how it can help you develop a growth mindset.

*Gratitude and Resilience*
Resilience is the ability to bounce back from adversity. It is a crucial skill to have in life because everyone faces setbacks and challenges at some point. Studies have shown that gratitude can increase resilience, making it easier to cope with difficult situations.

When you practice gratitude, you focus on the positive aspects of your life, even in the face of adversity. This helps you develop a more positive outlook and reduces the impact of negative emotions. By cultivating gratitude, you can develop the strength and resilience you need to overcome challenges and bounce back from setbacks.

### Gratitude and Motivation

Gratitude can also be a powerful motivator. When you focus on the positive aspects of your life, you feel more inspired and energized to pursue your goals. Gratitude can help you stay focused on the big picture and remind you of why you are working towards your goals in the first place.

For example, if you are working towards a promotion at work, it can be easy to get bogged down in the day-to-day tasks and lose sight of your overall goal. However, by practicing gratitude, you can stay motivated by focusing on the positive aspects of your job, such as the opportunity to learn new skills or the support of your coworkers.

### Gratitude and a Growth Mindset

Finally, gratitude can help you develop a growth mindset. A growth mindset is the belief that your abilities and intelligence can be developed through hard work and dedication. This is in contrast to a fixed mindset, which is the belief that your abilities and intelligence are fixed and cannot be changed.

When you practice gratitude, you focus on the progress you have made and the potential for growth in the future. This helps you develop a growth mindset and be more open to learning and developing new skills.

### Using Gratitude to Achieve Your Goals

Now that we understand the role of gratitude in increasing resilience, motivation, and a growth mindset, let's explore how we can use gratitude to achieve our goals.

First, identify your goals and the steps you need to take to achieve them. Then, use gratitude to help you stay motivated and focused on your progress. This can involve gratitude journaling, where you write down the things you are grateful for related to your goal or affirmations that reinforce your commitment to your goal.

For example, if your goal is to run a marathon, you might write down things you are grateful for related to running, such as the opportunity to be outdoors or the feeling of accomplishment after a long run. Maybe even the good health you'll be in to complete it! You might also repeat affirmations, such as "I am committed to training for my marathon and am grateful for the progress I am making."

By using gratitude to stay motivated and focused on your progress, you can increase your chances of achieving your goals and experience a greater sense of fulfillment and happiness along the way.

On this journey obstacles will exist. Those that often get in the way of developing a consistent gratitude practice but we will discuss the strategies for overcoming them.

**Obstacle 1:** *Lack of Time*
One of the most common obstacles to practicing gratitude is feeling like there's simply not enough time in the day. However, it's important to recognize that gratitude practice doesn't need to be time consuming. Even taking just a few moments each day to reflect on the things you're grateful for can have a significant impact on your well-being.

*Tip: Try setting aside a specific time each day to practice gratitude, such as first thing in the morning or before bed. This can help make it a habit and ensure that it doesn't get overlooked in the busyness of the day.*

**Obstacle 2:** *Lack of Motivation*
Another common obstacle to gratitude practice is a lack of motivation. It can be easy to get caught up in negative thoughts and feelings, making it difficult to focus on the positive.

*Tip: Try starting small and focusing on something that you're genuinely grateful for. This can help build momentum and motivate you to continue your practice.*

**Obstacle 3:** *Difficulty Seeing the Good*
Sometimes it can be challenging to find things to be grateful for, particularly during difficult times. It's important to remember that even small things can be sources of gratitude, such as a sunny day or a kind gesture from a friend.

*Tip: Make a list of things you're grateful for each day, even if they seem small or insignificant. Over time, this practice can help shift your perspective and make it easier to see the good in your life.*

**Obstacle 4:** *Life Challenges*
Finally, life challenges such as illness, financial struggles, or relationship issues can make it difficult to stay committed to a gratitude practice. During these times, it can be especially important to focus on the things you're grateful for, no matter how small they may seem.

*Tip: Try incorporating gratitude into your daily routine even during difficult times. This can help provide a sense of stability and perspective, making it easier to navigate life's challenges.*

*"Even though the day did not go as planned, I'm still thankful for (          )"*

By implementing these strategies and staying committed to your gratitude practice, you can overcome obstacles and reap the many benefits of gratitude in your life.

Gratitude can be a powerful tool for overcoming challenges and achieving your goals. By increasing your resilience, motivation, and developing a growth mindset, you can use gratitude to stay focused on the positive aspects of your life and maintain a sense of progress towards your goals. In the next chapter, we will explore how gratitude can enhance your relationships with others.

# IV

## Going Deeper with Gratitude

∞ ∞ ∞

Now that you have a basic understanding of ways to best use your gratitude, we will discuss how gratitude can be used to create a positive mindset, improve relationships, and manifest your desires. We will dive deeper into the practice of gratitude and explore some advanced techniques that can help take your gratitude practice to the next level.

*Creating a Positive Mindset:*
Gratitude can help shift our focus from the negative to the positive, creating a more optimistic and positive mindset. In this section, we will explore how to use gratitude to create a positive mindset and to reframe negative situations in a more positive light. We will also look at how practicing gratitude can increase our levels of happiness, positivity, and overall well-being.

*Deepening Relationships:*
Gratitude can also be used to deepen our relationships with others. In this section, we will explore how to use gratitude to improve our relationships with family, friends, and romantic partners. We will look at

how expressing gratitude can create a deeper sense of connection and intimacy in our relationships and how to practice gratitude in a way that is meaningful and impactful for our loved ones.

*Manifesting Your Desires:*
Gratitude can also be used as a tool to manifest our desires and achieve our goals. In this section, we will explore the concept of manifestation and how to use gratitude to attract abundance and prosperity into our lives. We will also look at some advanced techniques, such as visualization and gratitude rituals, that can help us manifest our desires more effectively.

*Taking Your Gratitude Practice to the Next Level:*
In this section, we will explore some advanced techniques that can help you take your gratitude practice to the next level. We will look at how to incorporate gratitude into your daily life in a more meaningful and intentional way and how to overcome any obstacles or challenges that may arise. We will also explore how to use gratitude to cultivate a deeper sense of purpose and fulfillment in your life.

Overall, this chapter will provide you with the tools and insights you need to take your gratitude practice to the next level and create a more positive, fulfilling life. By exploring the power of gratitude in a more in-depth way, you will be able to create more meaningful relationships, achieve your goals, and experience a deeper sense of well-being and fulfillment.

1. Cultivating a positive mindset with gratitude:

Gratitude is a powerful tool for cultivating a more positive mindset. When we focus on what we are grateful for, we shift our attention away from negativity and towards the good in our lives. This can help us to reframe our thoughts and adopt a more optimistic outlook.

As seen in Chapter 2, one way to use gratitude to cultivate a positive mindset is to keep a gratitude journal. This involves writing down three or more things you are grateful for each day. By focusing on the positive aspects of your life, you can train your brain to look for the good in any situation.

Another way to use gratitude to overcome negativity is to practice gratitude meditation. This involves sitting in silence and focusing your attention on your breath while also thinking about things you are grateful for. This can help to calm your mind and reduce feelings of anxiety or stress.

Finally, gratitude affirmations can also be a powerful tool for cultivating a positive mindset. By repeating positive statements about yourself and your life, you can reprogram your subconscious mind to focus on the good and attract more positive experiences into your life.

2. Deepening your relationships with gratitude:

Gratitude can also be a powerful tool for deepening your relationships with others. When we express gratitude to those around us, we strengthen our connections and build stronger bonds.

One way to use gratitude to deepen your relationships is to make a habit of thanking people for the things they do for you. This could be something as simple as thanking a coworker for their help on a project or thanking your partner for doing the dishes.

Another way to use gratitude to enhance your relationships is to practice active listening. This involves giving your full attention to the person you are talking to and expressing gratitude for the opportunity to connect with them.

Finally, gratitude can also be a powerful tool for forgiveness. When we express gratitude for the positive qualities in others, we can find it easier to forgive them for their shortcomings and focus on the good in our relationships.

3. Manifesting your desires with gratitude:

Gratitude can also be useful when manifesting your desires and achieving your goals. When we focus on what we are grateful for, we attract more of the same into our lives. This is the basis of the Law of Attraction.

One way to use gratitude to manifest your desires is to create a gratitude vision board. This involves creating a visual representation of the things you are grateful for and the things you want to attract into your life. By focusing on these positive images, you can attract more of the same into your life.

Another way to use gratitude to manifest your desires is to practice gratitude visualization. This involves visualizing yourself already having achieved your goals and expressing gratitude for them. By focusing on the feeling of gratitude, you can attract more of these positive experiences into your life.

Finally, gratitude can also be very powerful when setting and achieving goals. By expressing gratitude for the progress you have already made towards your goals, you can stay motivated and focused on your desired outcome.

4. Advanced gratitude practices:

For those who want to take their gratitude practice to the next level, there are a number of advanced techniques that can be used.

One such technique is the gratitude ceremony. This involves creating a ritual around your gratitude practice, such as lighting candles or burning incense. This can help to create a sense of sacredness around the practice and deepen your connection to the universe. You can also listen to soothing music when thinking of the things you're grateful for.

Another advanced gratitude practice is to participate in a gratitude challenge. This involves challenging yourself to express gratitude in a specific way, such as writing a letter of gratitude to someone (or yourself) each day for a week. By pushing yourself outside of your comfort zone, you can deepen your gratitude practice and attract even more positivity into your life.

Finally, combining gratitude with other practices such as meditation, visualization, and affirmations can amplify its power and help you achieve even greater levels of positivity and abundance in your life. Following this approach will take you steps closer to creating a powerful synergy between them and your gratitude practice.

When it comes to relationships, gratitude can be a powerful tool for deepening your connections and strengthening your bonds with the people in your life. By practicing gratitude for the people in your life, you are acknowledging and appreciating the positive qualities and experiences they bring to your life. This can help to cultivate a more positive and supportive environment, leading to stronger and more fulfilling relationships.

To apply this concept of gratitude to your relationships, take some time to reflect on the people in your life that you are grateful for. Think about the qualities and characteristics that you admire in them, the experiences you have shared, and the ways they have impacted your life for the better. Once you have identified these things, express your gratitude to them directly. You can do this through words, such as by telling them how much they mean to you, or through actions, such as by doing something kind or thoughtful for them.

When it comes to manifesting your desires, gratitude can be a powerful tool for attracting abundance and bringing your dreams into reality. By focusing on what you are grateful for, you are raising your vibration and attracting more positive energy into your life. This can help you to align with your desires and attract them more easily and effortlessly.

To use gratitude for manifesting, start by setting clear intentions for what you want to manifest in your life. Visualize yourself already having what you want, and feel the gratitude and joy that comes with it. Then, express gratitude for it as if it has already happened. You can do this through visualization, journaling, or affirmations. The key is to focus on the feeling of gratitude and allow it to shift your energy and vibration to attract what you want into your life.

# V

# Living a Grateful Life

∞ ∞ ∞

Congratulations on completing the previous chapters and committing to your daily gratitude practice. Now it's time to take your gratitude practice to the next level and integrate it into your daily life.

We will now recap how to express gratitude to others, how to find gratitude in challenging situations, and how to make gratitude a way of life.

### *Expressing Gratitude to Others*

One of the most powerful ways to live a grateful life is to express gratitude to others. Gratitude is contagious, and when we express our appreciation to others, we not only make them feel good but also elevate our own mood. Here are some practical tips on how to express gratitude to others:

1. Say "Thank You": This simple phrase is often overlooked but

can have a significant impact. Whether it's a coworker who helped you with a project or a friend who lent an ear, saying "thank you" goes a long way.

2. Write a Gratitude Letter: Take the time to write a letter to someone who has made a significant impact on your life. Be specific about the qualities you appreciate in them and how they have impacted your life.

3. Give a Small Gift: A small gift can be a tangible expression of gratitude. It doesn't have to be expensive, but it should be thoughtful.

## *Finding Gratitude in Challenging Situations*

Life is not always easy, and there will be times when we face challenges and difficulties. However, even in the midst of challenging situations, we can find things to be grateful for. Here are some tips on how to find gratitude in challenging situations:

1. Practice Mindfulness: Mindfulness is the practice of being present in the moment without judgment. When we practice mindfulness, we can find gratitude in the small moments of our lives, even in the midst of challenging situations.

2. Reframe Your Perspective: Try to reframe your perspective on the situation. Instead of focusing on what's wrong, try to find the silver lining and focus on what you can learn from the experience.

3. Practice Self-Compassion: Be kind and compassionate to yourself. Remember that everyone faces challenges, and it's okay to struggle. Practice self-care and gratitude for the things that are going well in your life.

## *Making Gratitude a Way of Life*

Finally, I will show you how to make gratitude a way of life. Here are some reminders on how to integrate gratitude into your daily life:

1. Keep a Gratitude Journal: Writing down what you are grateful for each day can help you focus on the positive things in your life.
2. Practice Gratitude Meditation: Take a few minutes each day to meditate on gratitude. Focus on the things you are grateful for, and allow yourself to feel the emotions associated with gratitude.
3. Use Gratitude Affirmations: Affirmations are positive statements that you repeat to yourself. By using gratitude affirmations, you can train your mind to focus on the positive things in your life.

When faced with difficult situations, our natural response may be to focus on what's going wrong and what we lack. This can lead to feelings of negativity, frustration, and despair. However, by shifting our perspective and looking for the silver lining, we can find gratitude even in challenging situations.

One way to find gratitude in difficult situations is to focus on what we have learned or gained from the experience. This can include personal growth, newfound strength, or a deeper appreciation for the people and things in our lives. We can also practice gratitude by finding the good in the situation, no matter how small. For example, if we are going through a health challenge, we can express gratitude for the medical care and support we have received, or for the moments of joy and connection we experience with loved ones.

Another way to find gratitude in challenging situations is to practice acceptance and surrender. This does not mean giving up or resigning ourselves to the situation, but rather acknowledging that it is a part of our journey and choosing to focus on the positive aspects rather than dwelling on the negative. We can use gratitude to reframe our perspective and see the situation as an opportunity for growth and learning.

Finally, it can be helpful to seek support from others and lean into our community during difficult times. By expressing gratitude for the people in our lives and the support they provide, we can cultivate a sense of connection and gratitude even in the midst of adversity.

In summary, finding gratitude in challenging situations requires a shift in perspective and a willingness to focus on the positive aspects of the situation. By looking for the silver lining, practicing acceptance and surrender, and seeking support from others, we can cultivate gratitude even in the midst of difficult circumstances.

We started our journey by understanding the power of gratitude and how it can help us cultivate a more positive mindset. We learned that practicing gratitude daily can help us reframe our thoughts and emotions, reduce stress, and improve our overall sense of wellbeing.

We then explored how to start our daily gratitude practice by identifying the things we are grateful for, keeping a gratitude journal, and practicing gratitude meditation. We learned that by consistently practicing gratitude, we can train our brains to focus on the positive aspects of our lives, and experience more joy and happiness.

Furthermore, we addressed common obstacles that people face when trying to cultivate a daily gratitude practice, such as lack of time or motivation. We shared some tips on how to overcome these obstacles and stay committed to our practice, even when life gets busy or challenging.

Moreover, we explored how to use gratitude to go deeper and experience greater transformation in our lives. We learned how to use gratitude to deepen our relationships, manifest our desires, and even find gratitude in challenging situations.

Finally, we discussed how to make gratitude a way of life. We learned the importance of creating a daily gratitude practice and how to incorporate gratitude into our daily routines. By making gratitude a habit, we can experience greater joy, fulfillment, and abundance in our lives.

Moving forward, use this guide as a roadmap for transforming your life through the power of gratitude. It is now up to us to take what we've learned in this book and apply it to our lives, one day at a time. As we continue to practice gratitude, we will experience greater transformation in our lives and live a more fulfilling life through gratitude.

# Epilogue

∞∞∞

Throughout this journey of learning and practicing gratitude, you've undoubtedly come a long way. You've learned about the science behind gratitude and how it affects our lives, you've started a daily gratitude practice, and you've faced and overcome obstacles along the way. It's important to take a moment to acknowledge and celebrate your progress and the growth you've experienced through-out this process.

Remember, cultivating gratitude is not always easy, and it takes time and commitment to see the benefits. But by taking the time to invest in yourself and your well-being through gratitude, you have already taken a powerful step towards living a more fulfilling life.

As you continue on your journey of gratitude, know that it's okay to make mistakes or have setbacks. The important thing is to keep going, to keep practicing, and to keep cultivating gratitude in your life. With each day, you have the opportunity to deepen your practice and experience the transformative power of gratitude.

So take a moment to reflect on how far you've come and feel proud of yourself for the progress you've made. And then, with renewed energy and determination, continue on your path of gratitude, knowing that the benefits will continue to grow and enrich your life.

# About the Author

Jess Williams is not only a successful songwriter, author, and public speaker, but a true inspiration to those seeking to overcome adversity and achieve their dreams. With a background in music and songwriting, Jess has performed for top brands worldwide and has used her platform to motivate and inspire others through her music and public speaking engagements, including captivating appearances at the iconic Howard Theatre in Washington DC.

Growing up in a single-parent home in South Central, Los Angeles, Jess faced numerous challenges and obstacles, but her determination and perseverance helped her overcome them all. Now, with her personal journey as a testament to her strength, Jess is dedicated to using her experiences and knowledge to guide others towards a more fulfilling life through gratitude.

Her book, "A Beginner's Guide to Daily Gratitude Practice," is a testament to her passion for personal growth and her desire to inspire others to live their best lives. With her words of wisdom and practical tips, Jess offers readers the tools to cultivate gratitude and transform their lives, one day at a time.

# Gratitude Journal

*Write or draw what you're grateful for.*

# Gratitude Journal

# Gratitude Journal

# Gratitude Journal

# Gratitude Journal

9 781088 129005